small worlds

IN A HOUSE

James W. R. Martin

CRABTREE
Publishing Company
www.crabtreebooks.com

Crabtree Publishing Company
www.crabtreebooks.com

PMB 16A, 350 Fifth Avenue
Suite 3308
New York, NY 10118

612 Welland Avenue
St. Catharines
Ontario L2M 5V6

CRABTREE:
Project editor: P. A. Finlay
Assistant editor: Carrie Gleason
Coordinating editor: Ellen Rodger

BROWN PARTWORKS:
Editor: Amanda Harman
Designer: Joan Curtis
Picture researcher: Clare Newman
Managing editor: Bridget Giles
Commissioning editor: Anne O'Daly
Consultants: Mark Hostetler, PhD, Assistant Professor, Extension Wildlife Specialist, IFAS,
University of Florida, and J. C. Lewis, PhD

Illustrator: Peter Bull
Photographs: Pascal Goetgheluck/Ardea p 16*m*; Steve Hopkin/Ardea p 8*m*; Jim Zipp/Ardea p 31; Dr. Eckart
Pott/Bruce Coleman Collection p 11; Kim Taylor/Bruce Coleman Collection p 10; Cereal Research
Centre/AAFC pp 7, 19*b/r*; Steve Austin/Corbis pp 5, 23; Hugh Clark/Corbis p 8*t/l*; Philip James Corwin/Corbis
p 30; Owen Franken/Corbis front and back cover, p 3; Gallo Images/Corbis p 22*m*; George Lepp/Corbis p 24; Joe
McDonald/Corbis pp 6*m/r*, 29*t/r*; The Purcell Team/Corbis p 4*m*; Galen Rowell/Corbis p 27; Scott T.
Smith/Corbis title page, p 28; Karen Tweedy-Holmes/Corbis p 9; Natural History Museum, London p 21*b*; N. A.
Callow/NHPA p 19*t/r*; Stephen Dalton/NHPA pp 6*m/c*, 6*m/b*, 7, 12, 14, 16*t/l*, 17, 20, 26*m*; Daniel Heuclin/NHPA
pp 13*t/r*, 13*b/r*, 29*b/r*; E. A. Janes/NHPA p 26*t/l*; Harold Palo Jr/NHPA p 4*t/l*; John Shaw/NHPA p 22*t*; Papilio
p 15; Cath Wadford/Science Photo Library front cover *b/r*, p 21*t*

Created and produced by
Brown Partworks Limited

First edition
10 9 8 7 6 5 4 3 2 1
Copyright © 2002 Brown Partworks Limited
Printed in Singapore

CATALOGING-IN-PUBLICATION DATA

Martin, James W. R.
  In a house / James W. R. Martin.
    p. cm. -- (Small worlds)
  Contents: Houses around the world -- The living house -- Sharing the house -- Finding food in the house --
Wood-munchers -- Fur, feathers, and scales -- What is living in your house?
  Summary: Describes the various animals that live in an old house in North America.
    ISBN 0-7787-0140-9 (RHC) -- ISBN 0-7787-0154-9 (pbk.)
    1. Household animals--Juvenile literature. [1. Urban animals. 2. Animals.] I. Title. II. Small Worlds (New York,
N.Y.).
  QL49 .G742 2002
  591.75'6--dc21
                        2001047295
                        LC

Contents

Houses around the world

People all around the world share their homes with many different animals, including mites, spiders, insects, mice, bats, and birds.

▲ *Barn owls sometimes nest in and around houses. They prefer quiet areas where they will not be disturbed by noise or people.*

▶ *Some birds, such as these starlings, often gather in large numbers on the roofs of houses.*

▶ *Spiders are common inhabitants of houses. Very few spiders are dangerous, and most are good to have around. House spiders catch and eat all kinds of house pests, such as flies.*

Many tiny animals find houses a good place to live. Houses provide shelter from hot weather or frosts and often provide a good source of food. Some larger animals also share our homes, using them as a safe place to hide during the day or as a spot to build their nests. In this book you will learn about some of the animals that live inside North American houses.

The living house

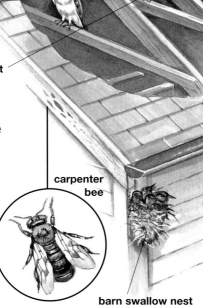

starling

paper wasp

barn owl

bat

carpenter bee

barn swallow nest

Most of the animals in our homes are active at night. During the day, they hide away in cracks, crevices, under carpets, and behind walls.

Many tiny animals such as insects feed on the leftover food in our garbage. Some eat natural fibers, such as wool and wood. Others feast on human blood, or the dead skin that our bodies shed. In turn, these tiny animals are eaten by larger animals such as spiders and centipedes.

Fur, feathers, and scales

A house provides a safe place for some larger animals. Birds make their nests on the roof, while house geckoes, rats, and mice search for food around the house at night.

Wood munchers

Insects such as beetles live in the wooden timbers of houses, as well as inside wooden furniture.

Finding food in the house

We share our food with many insects, including houseflies and cockroaches. They feed on our clothes, bedsheets, and even flakes of our skin!

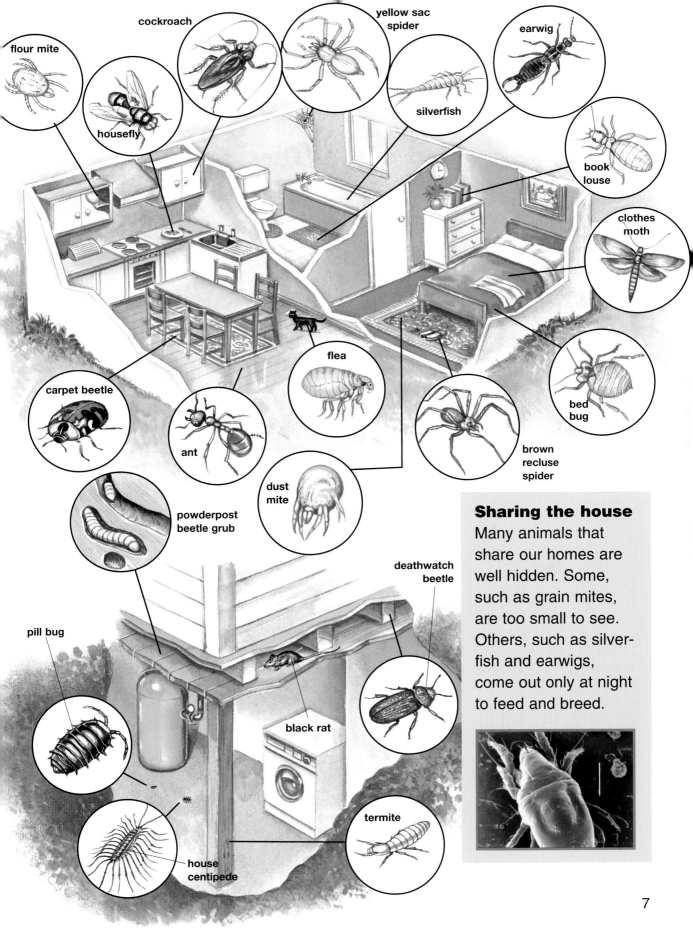

flour mite

cockroach

housefly

yellow sac spider

silverfish

earwig

book louse

clothes moth

carpet beetle

ant

flea

brown recluse spider

bed bug

dust mite

powderpost beetle grub

deathwatch beetle

pill bug

black rat

termite

house centipede

Sharing the house

Many animals that share our homes are well hidden. Some, such as grain mites, are too small to see. Others, such as silverfish and earwigs, come out only at night to feed and breed.

Sharing the house

Many animals prefer the quiet parts of the house, searching basements and garages for food during the day. Others explore sinks and tubs at night.

▲ *Like their close relations the silverfish, firebrats feed on starchy materials, such as breakfast cereals and wallpaper glue.*

▶ *Booklice are tiny gray or white insects. They eat starches in the pages of books and mold and fungi growing on old paper.*

Silverfish are tiny, wingless insects that live in cool, damp places, such as bathrooms. You can often see them moving around in bathtubs, where they search for food. In kitchens, they feed on starches such as cereals and flour. Silverfish are related to firebrats, which prefer warm, dark places, such as around fireplaces.

▶ *White-faced hornets are large, social wasps that often build their papery nests in and around houses. A nest can be 38 inches (97 cm) long.*

▼ *Female carpenter bees dig holes in wood and stuff them with pollen balls for their young to eat.*

Bees in the attic

Houses are safe from most predators and are good places to build nests. Sometimes, honeybee colonies split in two, and one swarm leaves to look for a place to build a new nest. The swarm sometimes rests on a branch or a fence post while scout bees look for a good site for the nest. Sometimes the bees head for a hole in the outside wall of a house, or even manage to get inside an attic, where they build a new nest.

Inside the nest, the bees use wax from their bodies to create many six-sided cells. They then fill some of the cells with sweet nectar, which they collect from flowers. The bees mix the nectar with spit and fan it with their wings to make honey. Other cells, called egg chambers, are used by the queen bee to lay her eggs. The honeybees work together to raise the young, gather food, and ward off enemies with their stingers.

Carpenter bees look like large honeybees but do not live in colonies. Each female carpenter bee raises a few young on her own. She makes her nest in the wood of porches and eaves.

Nests of paper

Unlike honeybee nests, wasp nests start with just a single queen. She builds her papery nest from saliva and chewed-up wood in a sheltered place, such as an attic, garage, or under the eaves of a house. Then, she begins to lay eggs in the nest cells to create a new colony of wasps.

▼ A wasp nest in an attic. The wasps come and go through the hole at the base of the nest.

Wasps feed caterpillars and other insects or spiders to the young. Each wasp colony lasts for just one year. In the fall, new queens leave the nest to mate. They take cover during the winter under tree bark, in holes in the ground, or sometimes in quiet parts of the house, before starting colonies of their own in the spring.

A mass of ants

Some types of ants make their nests in houses. They are drawn to warm places, such as around hot water pipes or inside walls. Like most house ants, little black ants feed on anything they can find. These insects nest in holes in wood and between bricks.

▼ Tiny pharoah ants are a big nuisance in houses, where they often live in large colonies of up to 300,000. They do not build nests but live in cracks and crevices.

Some ants leave scent trails for their nestmates to find food. Tiny odorous house ants get their name because they release a smell of rotting coconuts when crushed. Crazy ants are named because of the way they run around a room in search of food. Grease ants are named for the greasy meats and oils that they like to feed on in our kitchens.

Night hunters

Spiders usually avoid people but some use our homes as sheltered places to hunt and breed. House spiders are harmless to people but they are fierce **predators** of flying and crawling insects.

Many indoor spiders build webs made from lines of silk produced by structures called spinnerets on their abdomens. When an insect gets caught in the spider web, the insect's hairs stick to the silk.

Not all spiders use webs to catch their prey. Some spiders ambush cockroaches and other insects. They hide in warm places during the day and hunt at night.

FANTASTIC FACTS

● Spiders use tubular body parts, called spinnerets, to make their strong, sticky silk webs.

● Comb-footed spiders, including American house spiders, use their feet to gather strands of silk to throw over their prey.

Some spiders even live in shoes, clothes, or under people's bedsheets. If someone disturbs or threatens them, certain types of spiders will bite.

Wanderers from the yard

Female hobo spiders make webs in early summer. Soon after, male hobo spiders begin to search for mates. The males roam and enter homes looking for females. When frightened, these spiders often give a "dry bite," which is a bite without **venom**. Sometimes, hobo spiders do inject venom, causing great pain and even blood clots in humans.

In some parts of North America west of the Mississippi River, scorpions are also dangerous visitors to homes. During the day they hide in walls or small cracks in bricks. At night, they come out to hunt for food. Sometimes they search for water in kitchens and bathrooms.

▲ The brown recluse spider gives a nasty bite if it is disturbed.

▼ Female daddy longlegs spiders carry a sac of eggs in their mouthparts until the eggs are ready to hatch.

Spider hunters

Daddy longlegs spiders often live in dark places, such as attics and basements. They make their webs in the corners of walls and ceilings where they wait for prey to fly or walk into them. They are named for their long spindly legs.

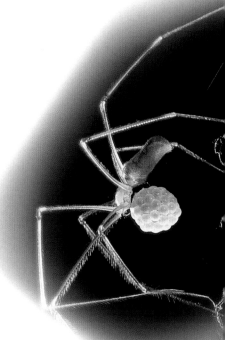

Daddy longlegs spiders look fragile, but they are fierce predators of other spiders. They will even attack a victim as it sits in its own web, throwing lines of silk to pin it down before giving a paralyzing bite. Daddy longlegs spiders are often confused with harvestmen (also called daddy longlegs). Harvestmen also have long spindly legs but cannot bite or spin webs and are neither insects nor spiders.

Leggy predators

Like spiders, house centipedes eat insects, including cockroaches. House centipedes can be up to one and a half inches (five centimeters) long, and have fifteen sections, each with a pair of long legs. These animals chase their prey and kill it by injecting venom through a pair of fangs.

▼ *Earwigs do not usually bite. They can be pests in large numbers.*

Earwigs under the carpet

Many animals live outside but come inside when the weather is bad. For example, very hot weather sometimes drives earwigs into houses in search of a cool place.

Earwigs prefer moist places. They hide during the day under rugs and carpets or in the gaps between floorboards. They come out at night to eat fruit, other insects, and sometimes the roots and buds of houseplants. Earwigs are usually brown or orange. Male earwigs have a long pair of pincers while the female's pincers are a little shorter.

▼ *Like other crustaceans, pill bugs molt, or shed, their hard outer covering as they grow. They molt the rear half first, then the front half.*

Crustaceans in the basement

Pill bugs and sow bugs are **crustaceans**, relatives of crabs and lobsters. Like other crustaceans, these animals breathe through **gills** rather than lungs. Gills need moisture to work, so pill

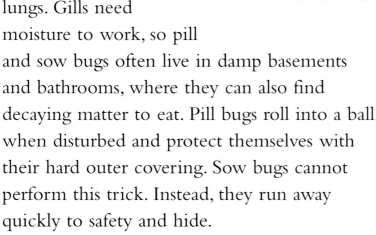

and sow bugs often live in damp basements and bathrooms, where they can also find decaying matter to eat. Pill bugs roll into a ball when disturbed and protect themselves with their hard outer covering. Sow bugs cannot perform this trick. Instead, they run away quickly to safety and hide.

Finding food in the house

Some of the small animals that live in our homes are considered pests. These tiny animals spoil food, eat clothes, and can spread diseases.

▲ *When they are caterpillars, brown house moths eat carpets and the fabric on furniture. Adult females can lay as many as 600 eggs during their lifetime.*

▶ *Mealworm beetles and their larvae eat cereal inside a cupboard. The paler "grubs" are really inactive* **pupae.**

Among the most hidden of all insects that inhabit our homes are cockroaches. These insects hide in cracks and crevices during the day but come out at night to feed. They eat almost anything, which makes trash cans popular sources of food. American and oriental cockroaches are the largest cockroaches found in our homes.

▶ *When cockroaches come out to eat, they sometimes leave their droppings on food. The insect dung contains germs that can spread diseases to people.*

Cockroaches measure around two inches (five centimeters) long. They are flat, brown insects with long antennae. Although they have wings, cockroaches usually do not fly when they are disturbed. Instead, they skitter away quickly across the floor. Oriental cockroaches live in damp, cool places, such as basements. The female cockroach carries about sixteen eggs in a sac for close to five days. Then, the mother cockroach leaves the egg sac next to some food so the newly hatched young can eat right away.

▼ There are four stages in the life cycle of a housefly: eggs, larvae, pupae, and adults. The complete cycle takes between 10 and 21 days, depending on the temperature.

Flying pests

Throughout spring and summer, houseflies fly into our homes through open windows to feed or lay their eggs. Flies often eat manure and garbage from outside, so when they land on human food inside the home they can spread germs and diseases. Houseflies taste food through pads on their feet. If they like what they taste, they spit out saliva, which turns the food to liquid. The flies then suck the food up with their spongy mouthparts.

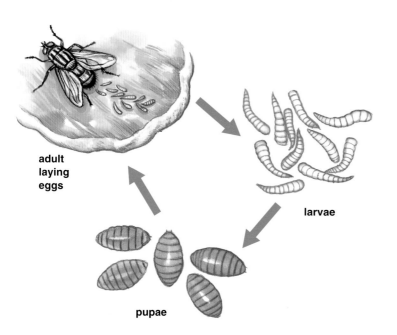

adult laying eggs

larvae

pupae

Tiny flies

The trash can is a popular place for many insects to live. Fruit flies often lay their eggs on rotting food. The grubs of these tiny flies breathe through a tube on their abdomens. They burrow into the garbage looking for yeast, a type of fungus found on decaying matter, to eat.

▲ *Fruit flies mating. In warm houses, their entire life cycle takes only eight days.*

▼ *This adult mealworm is a type of beetle.*

Mealmoths and mealworms

If you see tiny moths fluttering in a zigzag fashion around a cupboard at night, there might be a mealmoth colony nearby. Adult mealmoths lay their eggs in foods such as cereals, so that their young can eat the cereal. They leave behind strands of silk as they wriggle on the cereal, causing pieces of it to clump together. Dark cupboards with food inside are also a favorite habitat for mealworms. These long, thin, yellow beetle grubs, or **larvae**, look like small worms.

Chewing through clothing

Other moths that cause havoc in homes are clothes moths. Carpets and clothing that have been stored away are favorite foods of the grubs. Young webbing clothes moths hide under a cloak of silk and fibers to eat.

Feeding on humans

Insects not only steal our food, but some of them also feed on us! To grow, all insects and spiders must molt, or shed, their outer covering. Bed bugs, for example, molt five times before they become adults. Before **molting**, these insects need a meal of blood. Hiding away in cracks in walls, mattresses, and bed sheets during the day, bed bugs come out at night to drink blood from sleeping humans. Another group of tiny blood-drinkers are fleas. These insects sometimes live in the carpets and rugs of houses, especially those that are home to pet dogs or cats. Fleas are good jumpers, and they can leap a long way to land on a furry animal. Even smaller than these insects are dust mites, which feed on the skin that falls naturally from our bodies. These tiny animals live in large numbers. A single mattress can contain as many as 10 million of them!

Casemaking clothes moth larvae make silk tubes that they carry around with them while they feed. As adults, these tiny moths do not like light. When they are disturbed, they scurry away to a dark place, instead of flying away.

A bad habit

Some beetles are named after their favorite type of food. Cigarette beetles are pests of stored tobacco. They also eat wheat flour, seeds, and other dried plants. Drugstore beetles often eat medicines. These tough insects can even eat poisons without getting sick. Drugstore beetles hide during the day but come out at night to feed.

These insects lay different numbers of eggs. Cigarette beetles lay eggs in batches of 30 throughout the summer, while drugstore beetles lay only one egg at a time.

▲ *A drugstore beetle climbs onto a saccharin tablet. These tiny beetles eat a range of stored foods, as well as tobacco and drugs.*

Mighty mites

Insects are not the only animals that make a nuisance of themselves in kitchen cupboards. Several types of mites, such as grain mites and cheese mites, also live on human food. These tiny animals are just one fiftieth of an inch (half a millimeter) long. Although they are very small, their droppings and shed skin can cause allergic reactions in some people.

Mites are relatives of spiders and scorpions. They belong to a group of animals called arachnids. These tiny animals have eight legs. Insects, such as beetles and bees, have only six legs.

▼ *In large numbers, cheese mites, such as this one, can cause allergic reactions in people who touch the mites' food.*

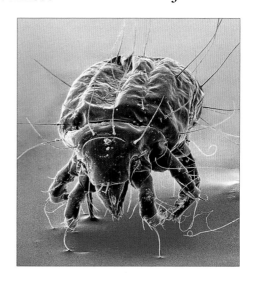

Wood munchers

Some insects chew through wood for food and to make their nests. They can cause great damage to houses and furniture.

▲ A carpenter ant carries eggs in her mouth. As many as 4,000 carpenter ants can live in a colony.

▶ These antlike insects are termites. They are easily recognizable because of their white bodies and brown heads. These workers are waiting for eggs to come out of the much larger queen's body (top right).

Among the most destructive wood eaters are insects called termites. Species such as the Eastern subterranean termite often make their colonies in the soil underneath houses. They build mud tunnels between the nest and their favorite food, wood. Worker termites slowly tunnel through the wood and can eventually cause a lot of damage to wooden house frames.

▶ The holes made by tunneling beetle larvae, or woodworms, destroy all kinds of wood, including furniture and house frames.

Big builders

Unlike termites, black carpenter ants do not eat wood, but they do tunnel through it. They build their nests in old or rotting timbers. There are two types of black carpenter ant workers. Large ones search for food, bringing insects and vegetable matter back to the nest to feed the colony. Smaller worker carpenter ants dig passages into the wood to make the nest larger. The ants dump small piles of sawdust, mixed with the outer coverings of dead insects, outside the nest.

Deathwatch beetles also tunnel through wood when they are grubs.

Digesting wood

Most insects and other animals are unable to digest wood and use it as food. Termites and some other wood eaters use tiny organisms in their bodies to convert, or change, the wood into food. These organisms break down the main part of the wood, called **cellulose,** into sugars, which the termites can digest.

Adult deathwatch beetles communicate by thumping their heads against the floor of their tunnels. These beetles are named for the eerie knocking sound this produces. People once believed that the rapping was heard when somebody in the household was going to die.

Powderpost beetles

Furniture made of hard woods such as oak or mahogany is often attacked by powderpost beetles. These insects get their name from the little piles of wood dust that build up outside the entrance to their tunnels. The adults chew a circular exit hole in the wood before flying away to mate and lay eggs on other pieces of wood.

The right kind of wood

Most tunnelers lay their eggs on the surface of the wood, leaving the young to munch away once they hatch. In the case of leadcable borers, the females even dig a tunnel before laying their eggs, giving the grubs a head start. It is important for these beetles to tunnel into the right kind of wood. They get their name because they will even bore through layers of soft metals and plaster in search of suitable egg-laying sites.

▲ *It can take as many as ten years for deathwatch beetle grubs to grow into adults. The life cycle of the deathwatch beetle moves from egg, to larva, to pupa, then to adult.*

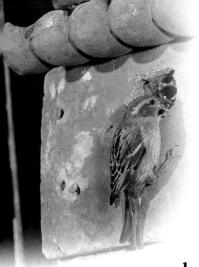

Fur, feathers, and scales

Occasionally you might end up sharing your house with large animals. Many species use houses to nest in or for shelter from bad weather.

▲ *Some house sparrows, brought to North America in the 1850s, make their own nest. Others take the empty nests of other birds such as swallows.*

▶ *Rats sometimes nest in houses. They can spoil food and spread diseases through their droppings, blood, and urine. Some even chew through electric cables.*

Rats and mice sometimes live under the floors of houses, as well as in drains and sewers. These rodents survive because of their diet. They will eat almost anything. Black rats and Norway rats are two species that occasionally live in our houses.

▶ *A peregrine falcon perches on a balcony. Falcons feel at home on high-rise buildings since their natural homes are cliffs.*

House mice make their nests from gnawed paper or fabrics.

Barn swallows use mud pellets to build cup-shaped nests under the eaves of houses.

The Norway rat has gray-brown fur and a long scaly tail. This rat can measure up to seventeen inches (46 cm) long. Black rats are a little smaller than Norway rats and have smooth, dark fur.

House mice live in small colonies, often in attics or basements. Other species of mice, such as deer mice and white-tailed mice, sometimes nest in quiet, sheltered parts of the house. These mice store seeds and berries close to their nests.

A good place for a nest

Many birds make their nests on or inside houses. Some birds, such as barn owls, often nest inside lofts and attics of old buildings. Other birds build nests on the roofs and eaves of houses. House sparrows build their untidy nests of straw and twigs in the corners of eavestroughs and on chimneys and roofs. European starlings are noisy birds that sometimes nest in great numbers. Unlike sparrows, they prefer to nest in cavities or holes in houses.

Plants, such as ivy, often grow on the walls of old brick houses. The dense tangle of leaves makes an ideal nest site for house finches and robins.

Bats in the attic

Not all flying visitors to the house are birds. Bats usually **roost** in cool, dry habitats such as caves or holes in large, old trees. Some bats spend the summer and much of the winter in the attics of houses, using them as sheltered places in which to raise their young. During the fall, the bats go into a long sleeplike state called **hibernation**.

Bats are helpful to humans, eating many pest insects in the summer. They are often seen swooping around the house in the evening sky.

▲ *Bats need places where they can be protected from frost to hibernate until spring. Attics are perfect for many species, such as these brown bats.*

House geckoes

House geckoes are lizards that live in houses in the warmer southern United States. They come out at night to eat insects. Their padded toes let them cling to smooth surfaces, so they can hunt their prey on walls and even on ceilings! During the day, the geckoes hide in houseplants or cracks in the wall. Each gecko chirps loudly to defend its own area in the house.

When they hatch from their eggs, house geckoes are tiny, measuring only 0.8 inches (two centimeters) long. Within a year, they grow quickly and reach about six inches (fifteen centimeters) long when fully grown. Geckoes do not have eyelids, so they lick the transparent covering of their eyes to keep them clean!

What is living in your house?

You do not need to visit an old house with creaking wood floors to find wildlife. Animals find warmth and safety in all types of buildings.

A good place to look for animals hiding during the day is in the attic or the basement. You can often find small animals, such as earwigs, centipedes, and pill bugs, under boxes and other places where it is dark and a little damp. These tiny nighttime animals avoid the light, where they are more easily detected by predators. Be ready for them to scurry away in a hurry!

You can often see the work of wood-boring beetles in old furniture and other wood objects around the house. Look for the tiny holes where the beetles have gnawed their way out of the wood.

▲ *Insects, such as this ladybug, often wander or fly into houses from the outside.*

▶ *A quiet place on the side of the house is a good place for a birdhouse. You might persuade a bird to nest in it. This eastern bluebird is entering its new nest.*

If birds make a nest on or near your roof, you can see the parent birds as they fly in with food. Many birds, such as barn swallows, appear regularly with their beaks full of flies and other insects for their young. If your attic is home to a small colony of bats, you might have the chance to observe their habits. If you can find where the bats leave the attic to feed in the evenings, try counting the bats to see how many are roosting there. Half an hour before and after sunset are the best times to look.

TOP TIPS FOR HOUSE DETECTIVES

1 The best way to look at small animals without hurting them is through a magnifying glass. Use a pair of binoculars to watch birds.

2 Try not to attract pest animals indoors. Instead, leave a small piece of fruit outside. Insects such as fruit flies will be attracted to it.

3 Ask an adult to help you lift boxes in basements and attics. You might find animals such as centipedes and pill bugs living underneath.

Words to know

Cellulose The tough part of wood and other plant material.
Crustacean A type of animal, such as a crab or shrimp, that has jointed limbs, two pairs of antennae, and a hard outer skin. Most live in water.
Gill A feathery organ that some animals use to breathe.
Hibernation A deep "sleep" during the winter months.

Larvae Immature insects.
Molting Shedding skin, hair, or feathers ready for new growth.
Predator An animal that hunts other animals for food.
Pupa Stage when a larva changes into an adult insect.
Roosting Resting at night (birds) or during the day (bats).
Venom Poison injected by some hunting animals, such as spiders.

Index